Digital Marketing
Manual

Will Rowan

I0475003

The Digital Marketing Manual
Published 2011

First published 2000 as
The eCommerce Pocketbook.
Reprinted 2003.
Second edition published 2006.

ISBN: 1461004780
ISBN-13: 978-1461004783

for Sue, without whom...

"Will's a thought leader in taking the internet to the wider world, the idea to the business and the geeks to the market. He's grounded in reality while at the same time able to imagine where you could and should be several years from now. If you're looking at how to engage the web and translate your offline success to the on, Will's your man."

James Farmer, Online community expert, founder Edublogs.org & WPMUdev.org

"Talk about Savvy; Will Rowan knows his stuff, and is always cutting edge. He makes sure you do the simple things right, and do them well, but will also leave you hungry for more keeping the bigger picture at the forefront of your mind."

Linley Lewis, Founder, Ticket To Ride ttride.com

"An hour spent with Will will give you a supply of useful things to think about for a week. Friendly, frank and open, he introduces you to possibilities and perspectives that you might never have thought of, in a way that helps you integrate them into your programme as if they had been there all the time. It's amazing how many brilliantly original ideas you come up with while Will is sitting with you not appearing to do much."

Malcolm Sleath, Owner & principal coach 12boxes.com

"Few people truly understand the challenges and opportunities of digital marketing. Will is one of those few - a pathfinder in the networked economy."

Ian McDonald Wood FutureValue.co.uk

CONTENTS

Be Informative ⇒ Level Three: Easier Sales Cut Friction & Add Profit On Every Sale ⇒ Cater For Everybody, Not Just Online Customers ⇒ Level Four: Be Sociable

5 EFFECTIVE EMAIL MARKETING

Managing Permission Email ⇒ Email Is Not All About Words ⇒ Three Types Of Email ⇒ Email Design ⇒ Compelling Email Copy ⇒ Using Email Signatures Effectively ⇒ Business To Business Email Guidelines

6 SOCIAL MEDIA & ONLINE PUBLIC RELATIONS

Adding Social Content ⇒ Opinion Formers ⇒ Keep It Real & Personal ⇒ Who Matters? ⇒ Automated Updates ⇒ Newsgroups & Message Boards ⇒

7 DIGITAL ADVERTISING

Four Forms Of Online Advertising ⇒ Buying And Publishing Online Advertising ⇒ Using Cookies To Make Display Advertising Relevant

8 MANAGING SEARCH ENGINES

Getting The Best From Search Engines ⇒ Seven Important Tag Concepts ⇒ Accessible Pages Are Easy To Spider ⇒ Where Do Visitors Come From? ⇒ What Do Visitors Do On Your Site? ⇒ Well-networked Pages Get More Traffic ⇒ Update Pages Regularly To Keep Them Visible ⇒ Use Customer Service To Support Visibility ⇒ Learn From Competitors! ⇒ Just A Few Measurements ⇒ And Finally, Momentum

9 MANAGING CUSTOMER SERVICE TO CREATE TRUST

Make Your Security Appropriate ⇒ Secure Your Site Internally & Externally ⇒ Website & Visitor Verification ⇒ Customer Transaction Records ⇒ Trust ⇒ Five Ways To Build Trust Online ⇒ 1. Consistent Presentation ⇒ 2. Visitors Decide Navigation Priorities ⇒ 3. Transparent Fulfillment ⇒ 4. We Trust Familiar Names & Logos ⇒ 5. Use As Little Technology As Possible ⇒ Six Ways To Lose Customer Trust ⇒ Data Protection ⇒ Collecting & Using Impersonal ⇒ Data At A Single Site ⇒ Actions To Protect Data That Is Gathered Online

10 EIGHT GOOD PLANNING STEPS

1 let the customer plan digital marketing
2 respond fast
3 test out your plan
4 challenge internal assumptions
5 focus on customer, supplier & distributor benefits
6 give good reasons to use online services
7 calculate three sets of costs
8 help staff adapt to online working

ACKNOWLEDGMENTS

In over a decade's worth of conversations, chats over coffee (beer & wine), networking events and reading, it would be impossible to individually thank everybody who's shared a thought. Large & small, they've all contributed.

Recent influencers include the members of LikeMinds, Mashup & VRM london.

And of course my clients, without who so many ideas would stay intangible thoughts.

CHAPTER 1
WHAT IS DIGITAL MARKETING?

A moment of calm in the storm to a networked, online world

In the rush to digitize businesses, it's all too easy to forget that the human beings this side of the screen won't change much.

Some have adapted early and have already leapt online.

Others will take longer.

And some of us will never wish to go online.

In the dash to offer online services to your customers, never forget that some of them just don't want to come and play.

WHAT NOT TO EXPECT

Don't expect to gain an advantage just by being online

Don't dress up an existing business with a dot.com façade

Don't use it as an alternative to investing in sound customer service

Don't think only of reaching the internet on a PC: our cell phones, tablets, televisions and games consoles are online too

Don't take short cuts; it might look the same but won't get the same results

Don't think that spending more to develop a digital presence will automatically make more money

And don't expect:

Digital Marketing to happen quietly, in a corner, over there behind the shrubbery

To keep the rest of your business unchanged

To be an overnight success

WHAT'S DRIVING Digital Marketing growth?

Every day more people are online - at home and at work, via computers, telephones and televisions. These devices are becoming faster, smarter and are connecting to each other.

For many items that we need to buy, both domestic and commercial, online is a more convenient way of shopping.

The businesses that sell to us can reduce their costs, making each sale more profitable.

A DEFINITION OF Digital Marketing

By connecting to standardized networks we can find information, buy, sell & promote quickly and easily, with lower process and administration costs.

WHAT'S GROWING THE DIGITAL POPULATION?

The long answer: Everything's connected

The phones we carry in our pockets, our tablets, laptops, computers and even TV screens are networked. And they're synchronized - and as we swap devices we're far more likely to carry on what we were doing if we can pick up where we left off.

The short answer: Facebook

It's not the only social network, but when half a nation's population has an account, then you'd have to think that Facebook features in many folks' lives.

The cost of being connected is falling, fast.

Moore's Law holds that every 18 months computing power halves in cost (or doubles in power). This means that we get mobile telephones with more power than ten-year old computers.

Almost every computing device is connected to a network - wired into an office network, or connected to the internet.

Smartphones are becoming commonplace.

Our phone networks were mostly built to carry voice calls. Now the majority of traffic is not voice but data.

Our next phone networks will deliver true broadband to mobile devices; widespread WiFi networks in cities will share the network load.

First Blackberrys showed that you could deal with email on your mobile, then the iPhone put a browsable internet in your hand. Android phones brought the price down.

Far from just being able to work while on the move, social stuff - Facebook - has given many folk a reason to want the internet on their phone.

FOR READERS WORKING TO INTERNET TIME

7 things to know about digital marketing

1. Online, space is practically infinite; the value of space falls as the supply rises

2. Successful digital marketing takes costs out of business processes

3. It's possible to be open 24/7/365

4. Distance disappears when connections are electronic and online

5. Company size is not a competitive advantage when everybody is on the same screen

6. Heritage, and the customer perceptions it brings, may be a disadvantage

7. Relationships matter even more online

Action Plan
8 things to do

1. Take costs out of your existing business

2. Improve your internal communications

3. Build a community and get knowledge to flow freely inside and outside

your company

4. Make external communications more cost-effective

5. Find more efficient ways to reach existing customers

6. Take orders 24 hours a day

7. Exploit the opportunities created by being closer to all of your customers

8. Try out new markets with less risk

And one thing not to do:

Don't bet the company on an online venture.

Internet time is said to run seven times faster. One internet month, therefore, is equivalent to seven 'real' months.

Like dogs.

Make of that what you will!

8 What is Digital Marketing?

CHAPTER 2

THE FIVE BUSINESS BENEFITS OF
DIGITAL MARKETING

1. CUT COSTS, NOT SERVICE

Cutting the cost of making a sale is the next best thing to a price rise. And unlike a price rise, customers don't notice cost-cutting (when it's done right)!

So-called frictionless trade benefits the entire business by getting computers to handle processing and information tasks for your whole business, online and offline. Information need only be entered into a system once. In that case it had better be correct.

Your customers are the best people to get much of the information onto your systems correctly, first time.

We all know how to spell our own details and it matters to us that they're right.

Use the internet to save money by out-sourcing data entry to your customers.

And beware of using digital marketing only to save money.

Beware of using digital marketing only to save money.

Yes, I said that in the previous paragraph
so it must be important.

Your customers' expectations will change, so reinvest your savings in customer service because:

✦ the web's transparency means that inadequate service shows up fast.

When customers can't find information for themselves online, they'll want answers quickly from your support staff. Bad news can travel very fast online: a web community can let a whole industry know of a problem, quickly.

✦ aim for faster customer service and move it online for greater cost-effectiveness

✦develop online self-help customer service for simple, routine questions. Save staff resources for tougher, one-off customer concerns

✦be prepared to re-train your customer service teams. They will be answering much more detailed questions from your online customers.

2. MEASURE TO MAKE DECISIONS

Online, everything can be measured.

Everything that happens online can be tracked, counted and measured. The details are usually held in a log file[1] available from the host computer.[2] it's a goldmine of information on how your customers use your online channels:

✦ who came in & where they came from

✦ routes taken around the site

✦ products looked at

✦ products bought

This information is virtually free to collect. The challenge is to find the information that will inform management decisions.

Measure traffic for quantity and quality.

Do you have plenty of online visitors? Are they the right people?

Most visitors will not tell you exactly who they are, unless they need more information from you.

But you **will** be able to see:

✦ where in the world they came from

✦ which internet service providers are most common: local, national or international

✦ what time of day your site is busiest

---

[1] A log file reports (logs) activity on your website.

[2] The host computer stores your website. It is often an internet service provider or another host.

Don't mistake a high volume of traffic for valuable traffic. What use are overseas shoppers if you only deliver locally? They will only soak up valuable company resources that you need for local customers.

Where do visitors come from?

How did your visitors find you? If you know that, there's more chance of encouraging more folk to visit.

Websites sit on servers whose log files have all the traffic reports that could be used to analyze and manage the flow of visitor traffic through a site. But you'll never look at them!

Check out the few records that matter:

- ✦ do you know visitors already?
- ✦ is it their first visit or are they returning?
- ✦ did they use a bookmark or did they find you through a search engine, or social network?
- ✦ what search terms did they use?
- ✦ which network sent them?

Browsers are the programs used to view the web. The most common three are Microsoft's Internet Explorer, Firefox and Apple's Safari

- ✦ which browser & which version are they using?
- ✦ do pages display as you meant them to?
- ✦ what are the top screen resolutions?

Look at the routes taken by visitors:

◆ did visitors find what they were looking for?

◆ did visitors do what **you** wanted them to?

Spending the right amount of time on a page

Which was the first (entry) page to your site? Search engines won't always lead surfers to your home page. If one page is particularly popular, try to understand why.

◆ what are the most popular routes?

◆ which pages do visitors link together?

◆ is that where you want them to go?

If it isn't, where is the smartest place to put a signpost link, to redirect the traffic flow?

Stickiness: which pages do visitors spend most time on? Was it finding product information, filling out forms and placing orders? Do they spend seconds or several minutes on these pages?

◆ is there a popular last page visited?

◆ what route do most visitors take when leaving your site? With luck, it will be the order page.

Track back visitors' routes to the exit pages. If those aren't the pages you'd like them to leave from, eg:

"Thanks for your purchase/inquiry/ registration"

then change the links and signposts to re-route them towards those preferred exit pages.

3. INTERACT TO ENGAGE

Human beings are naturally curious. We like picking up stones to see what's underneath, and we like clicking buttons and switches to see what happens. Websites are great at interactivity.

Use them to create immediate interest for your visitors.

Have your visitors interact with your pages, to enable them to find the information that's really relevant to them today.

Facebook status updates, tweets, news items, photos and video are all simple, self-energizing nuggets that show a business' human face, and keep visitors up to date.

By clicking on content, visitors engage and involve themselves in discovering your products. In this way they'll spend longer at your site, and will tell you more about their interests through the pages that they look at.

While you're busy giving all those status updates & tweets, remember that you're here for a reason
– to get folk interested in what you do.

When adding social update to pages, beware of giving too much emphasis to them. Too many complex external graphics can slow down page load times, and are can be distracting. Pages should communicate first and entertain second.

4. PERSONALIZE TO ADD RELEVANCE

Interactivity drives personalization.

Isn't it nice when we visit a shop and are greeted by name? We feel recognized and valued.

Online, this applies too:

Shopkeeper: "Hi. Have you been before?"

Customer: "No"

Shopkeeper: "Let me give you the grand tour. Or was there something specific I can get for you?"

Alternatively, the customer answers "Yes" to the original question, in which case the shopkeeper says:

"What did you like? Can I show you that first next time?"

In this way the shopkeeper is given permission to get into conversation with the customer about who they are and what goods they like.

Personalization works for me.

Now that our customer is engaged in conversation the shopkeeper can ask the questions that drive personalization. It's the first step to free, accurate data collection.

To encourage folk to give out personal information, use the information they give!

There is no point asking for information that won't be used and that your visitors won't find interesting or won't useful.

There are three levels to personalization:

1 <u>Recognition</u> can save re-entering names and invoice and delivery addresses in order forms. This saves time and is convenient for customers.

2 Using software, the site can be personalized for the customer according to his or her past site activities.

3 The most advanced level is customization. Customers can choose how and when they view the site's content.

When visitors feel valued, they will return more frequently and stay longer each time.

Log in credentials: keep it simple!

Your business is not a bank, so it doesn't need multi-layer security processes.

Let customers choose their username and password: better still, let them use an email address as their username.

Don't force visitors to remember a random character sequence as their password; it'll only end up with them re-registering, or shopping elsewhere.

The simplest information to ask for is an email address. Give visitors sound reasons to share their email addresses. For example, tempt them with a newsletter, product updates and offers available only to registered visitors.

Don't ask visitors for unnecessary information.

While it may be in their interest to give some details - to make sure they get the right offers, for example - it's best to keep more detailed questions for later.

Personalization: automated by site software.

Online channels are good at managing information in order to automate tasks. First, though, they need information to manage.

Many websites work by placing short text messages (cookies) on the visitor's computer.

Usually cookies exist only to track the site visit and to help the website recognize a visitor's computer - not **who** is sitting at the keyboard, unless the user chooses to reveal this information.

Many cookies self-delete at the end of a browsing session. Others - persistent cookies - stay on the visitor's machine to recognize them on their next visit, and to remember their preferences.

Without cookies we would all find the internet much slower. However, some people are rightly concerned at their browsing information being captured and available for later use. So it's important to have a link to your privacy policy visible each time a form ask for personal information, and again at the foot of each page.

Customization: <u>by</u> visitors to <u>their</u> preferences.

Visitors may wish to customize the pages that they see, to make them as useful as possible.

Most of your customers will buy only some of your items. By personalizing page contents to their own preferences, visitors see only those products that they're most interested in.

Imagine, for example, a recipe book containing only your favorite foods plus some suggestions from the chef of similar dishes that you might like. Or a clothes catalogue that shows only clothes that fit!

Cookies make this possible on the simplest of websites.

Personalization should be a win-win for customer and company.

If customers are able to put together their own orders, then personalization will:

- Make it quicker and easier for the customer to buy in the future by showing only relevant products and by not asking for delivery and payment instructions to be re-entered.

- Make it less likely that customers will try out your competitors who offer less personalization - or, even, the same personalization opportunities - because they will have to re-enter their details.

- Reduce the cost of managing your customer accounts, by giving them access to their account information and allowing them to carry out much of their own account management.

5. GLOBAL REACH: LOCAL IMPACT

If your company's products can be distributed globally, then digital marketing channels are an excellent and efficient way to exploit them:

✦ new customers and markets @ $zero incremental set-up costs

✦ 24 hour sales presence

✦ distance is potentially irrelevant

✦ smaller product niches become profitable when the niche expands globally

All of which helps highly dispersed communities of customers to become closer to each other and to your organization.

& if products can't be distributed globally, don't waste time & valuable energy building (for example) a world-wide Twitter following!

Instead, keep your online presence local and useful;

✦ show maps, with address details & satnav coordinates in the sidebar

✦ publish a Booking diary, showing free/busy periods - and let customers at least make booking enquiries

✦ better still, let them make provisional bookings.

Either way, you now have the contact details of a prospective customer.

ACTION PLAN QUESTIONS TO ADDRESS

Prioritize the 5 business benefits by answering these key questions:

1 Where am I now on each benefit?

2 What are my customers doing online now, at my website and at my competitors' sites?

3 What impact will digital marketing have on my business:
- reducing costs?
- the flow of information to customers?
- the flow of information from customers?

4 What needs urgent attention and are these complementary activities?

5 How far, and how fast, should developments be made?

CHAPTER 3

NEW THINKING FOR ONLINE BUSINESS

YOUR CUSTOMER HAS MORE CONTROL

The network economy's logic is different from that of the high street. It's more important that your business is easy to find, trustworthy, and easy to buy from - and it's worth investing to make online services useful.

But don't, of course, ignore business basics such as profit & cashflow. Spend wisely - or not at all.

Human attention is the rarest commodity: customers respect, applaud and share content that's worthy of their attention - regardless of whether it's promoting a company.

If customers' attention is on networks, shape your marketing to their networks.

In the good old days, your customers were at the end of a chain that began in a factory and ended when they collected goods from shops.

Now, the online customer sits at the centre of a circle and is probably able to reach any part of the old distribution chain, in one step.

Being online gives customers much more choice over what they buy and control over who they buy from.

On the high street money is the currency that drives growth.

To secure more customers, businesses spend money to invest in stock or production capacity in readiness for more new customers. And more money is spent on advertising, to attract more customers, and on providing more customer service to a larger number of customers.

Don't forget too that on the high street prime locations cost more.

ONLINE, VISITOR ATTENTION DRIVES GROWTH

Online, visitor attention drives business growth, not money. There are three reasons why:

1. Offline it costs money every time you communicate with your customers: online this cost all but disappears. So it's less expensive to build customer loyalty online. And, as we all know, keeping an existing customer is more profitable than replacing a lost one.

2. Happy, interested customers are likely to tell others of their buying experiences. Virtuous circles develop faster online because it's quick, inexpensive and easy to contact friends and colleagues. Web people used to call this viral marketing - now it's developed into social media.

When customers use social media services, then maybe your company should be there too.

And if competitors use those social services to sell, that would be another reason to investigate how sociable your customers are.

It's simple & free to set up a survey, and ask!

3. Once the first online shop is built for online Customer Number 1, the running cost of providing the shop to Customer Number 2 through infinity is incrementally small - and the cost only arises when the sale is made. Online businesses should handle more orders for less processing cost and more profit.

There must be a catch?

You're right - there is. It's Returns.
A higher proportion of your online customers will return goods to you. They bought, tried them on, and sent them back. Expect anything up to 20% returns.

Make it as easy as possible for them to do that - though for lower cost goods, the customer should probably pay the postage cost of the return (but not of restocking).

If customers can quickly & easily fix their mistakes, and the business makes it a pleasure... there's every chance that customer will speak positively of your firm, and buy again.

The returned stock can most often be placed in a B Grade stock category, and sold at a slight discount... but probably still priced to make a profit.

STARTING A SOCIAL CAMPAIGN

Social, viral, "Word of mouth marketing,' ... call it what you will. It is the most trusted and low cost way to promote your business.

When customers recommend your business to their network, their endorsement adds trust to your marketing messages.

But first, customers need a product or service that they can recommend:

✦ an easy-to-browse, personalized catalogue

✦ ordering and account management tools

✦ online product manuals that are always up-to-date

Now, make it easy for customers to tell their friends - embed social network service links on every web page and in every email.

CREATING A SOCIAL NETWORKING CAMPAIGN

OK, so you've created a new service. What now?

Expensive old economy thinking would be to invest money and promote it.

Instead of giving customers advertising to look at, give them something that costs the business virtually nothing, and that customers will find useful.

That might be a light version of your service, if it's digital. Or a trial. Or the benefit of your expertise. Make it something worth talking about. Worth sharing with friends & colleagues. Something valuable.

Give away your new service.

In the old economy, companies charge more for products and services that are new and better. They charge a premium for the best.

When customers use the new service, they will bring in new customers. The more customers that use the service, the more new customers they will bring in. And sales will grow faster.

MAKE YOUR CUSTOMERS' LIVES EASY

Your customers' computer screens are busy places, and it's easy for customers to become distracted - so make your site and services easy to use. The less time it takes to buy, the less chance there is of being distracted.

1 Start every new service with a small-scale trial version.

2 Find out what customers like and use.

3 Improve the service regularly - little & often.

4 Use customer feedback in your improvement process: form a Beta test group of trusted customers and ask them to test new things ahead of their release.

5 Above all, make life easy for your customers. Use conventional layouts, standard checkout processes, and confirm every purchase by email.

Invite visitors and customers to share products, pages, and news from your business with their social networks. On every page. After every purchase. Folk love to share the things they've found.

FEEDING YOUR NETWORK TO GROW YOUR BUSINESS

Every person on one network is also part of other networks. At work there are colleagues, suppliers and customers, and away from the workplace we all have networks.

Once you've given away your new standard in order to build your network, how does the network grow?

Give away some more.

If the things that are given away are valuable to the network, then these people are likely to pay for the complementary services that are paid for. Which means that the more you give away, the larger your network and the more you'll sell.

Remember to give away things that:

✦ cost nothing to give away

✦ cost next to nothing if one more customer uses them

✦ build the network of paying customers.

In the old world way of marketing, companies spent money on marketing things - "collateral"- on advertising campaigns & promotional discounts - to get a message out to prospective customers. The idea was that marketing campaigns could change folks' attitudes & opinions, persuading them to buy a different product.

We're shown so many of these clever campaigns, from such a young age, that they're often filtered out. The marketing that makes its way past our filters is as likely to be viewed as art or entertainment as it is to persuade us to change our minds.

FOLK DON'T FILTER FRIENDS' MESSAGES

The new way of marketing is to give customers no-brainer reasons to do something: to share the idea with friends, to reply, or to buy.

The focus is less on sales, and more on sharing reasons to take a look at the company. We're naturally sociable creatures. Show us something interesting, and we'll want to have it, share it, use it. These are proven direct marketer's tried-and-tested Member Get Member programs principles, applied in a digital context.

We're far more likely to share relevant marketing with our friends. When customers self-target to shared affinities, it's with far greater accuracy than marketers' data models, because we tend to socialize with like-minded folk. And messages received from our trusted network of friends are themselves much more trusted than the same things when they're said by a company spokesman.

Social campaigns are a much simpler, much more direct approach to promoting products.. Faster. Easier to get done.

SOCIAL WORKS BEST ON A SMALL SCALE

...which is easier for smaller businesses to figure out, because they're already small scale. Big business has to work very hard at thinking small, thinking simply.

Cut out the campaign cost, and pass the value straight to where it will have most impact - with customers. In simple language that they'll get.

And share.

SET NEW STANDARDS

Be first with an idea and it will spread more rapidly. Set a new standard in your market (in your network) and gain a reputation as leader. As a company that's interesting to follow.

The formula is simple:

1. Start small, try out ideas and move on quickly.
2. Find out what customers like and use.
3. Improve things regularly, a little at a time.

Being first is nice, but far from essential.

Being the biggest player is one way of being important to customers, and of course it's not an option available to most businesses. Being friendly & available *is* a pitch that the smallest, local business can beat the largest of High Street names.

It's better for a company to be relevant to the folk they'd like as customers - which they can do by being friendly, available, and responsive.

Then it is much more difficult for competitors to break emotional ties to customers' favorite name companies.

THE NETWORK IS THE BEST JUDGE OF A GOOD IDEA

If you were allowed more than one smart idea, how many would you try?

As many as possible!

It is tough to know what customers will want, online or offline. And not every great idea is going to succeed. Give customers as many good ideas as possible - even not-quite-finished ideas.

The web has created the Beta version - a nearly-finished idea that companies try out on customers. You can try it out too. Customers feel recognized and rewarded when asked to be involved in product development. You get free market testing.

Some ideas will turn out to be less-smart or too complex to finish, so drop them.

HOW TO STAY AHEAD OF ONLINE COMPETITION

The internet is a great way of developing a business. Sadly, the competition can benefit from it too. Like you, competitors just need a great idea and a network to sell into.

To stay in front of them become your own best competitor. Don't only look to improve your products, try to make them obsolete with even better, new offerings.

Be prepared to let go of a product when it is at its most successful - and transfer its fan network to your new product.

ORGANIZING AROUND THE CUSTOMER

Companies structure themselves around products:

Management structure

Production and sales teams

Distribution channels

Traditional marketing is formed around four Ps:

Product

Place

Price

Promotion

for which it's fair to substitute the four main areas of traditional business organizations:

Manufacturing
    Distribution
        Accounting
            Sales

Customers don't think this way.

Never have done, never will do.

Customers think about the end product.
    "What do I get?"

Customers are interested in the meal, not the raw ingredients. Each individual product ingredient is a small part of the whole. Online, it is really easy to gather the whole buying experience onto one screen.

When Apple launched the iPod in 2001, with shuffle, listeners could hear music in any order they wished. Overnight, the artist & music company lost a significant piece of control over their product.

Music was suddenly organized the way that listeners wanted it.

It's smarter to organize online business around the way that customers think.

ONLINE SERVICES FOR ALL YOUR CUSTOMERS

Traditional supply chains deliver High Street goods via manufacturers, wholesalers and retailers. The web cuts through that supply chain, and customers can buy direct from any business in the chain.

Large and small customers may be using the same shop, but they need not see the same trading terms:

Prices can be lower for high volume, repeat customers

Where as individual sales will be paid for immediately and by credit card, business customers can enjoy longer payment terms

Bulk orders might receive packaging and delivery tailored to their needs

TEST ONLINE MARKETPLACES BEFORE BUILDING YOUR OWN SHOP

Businesses don't have to build their own shops to trade online - they can use a service which handles promotion, payments, and some customer support, for a commission on each sale:

Auction services - eBay is the biggest, but niche sites might work better for your company - allow fixed price and auction sales.

Each transaction adds to buyer and seller reputations: that reputation is a valuable asset - show it off everywhere your company trades.

Implant stores provide all the tools needed to set up a store. They may also offer production facilities. And will handle transactions - which can be very convenient, since that's often one of the slower parts to getting set up.

Quick & usually free to set up, these stores can bring footfall to your store. They'll charge a percentage on sales to cover their costs. Amazon's Z Shops & Ebay stores are largest; many niche specialists offer comparable services, and may have a better audience.

Co-buying services match buyers and sellers so that prices and cost of sale are reduced

Before investing in your own shop, try selling through one of these existing marketplaces, to see what benefits an in-house system will bring.

Drip drip drip

works way better than one big blast... which will be gone by next week. Build social networks one day at a time, listening to the response as you go.

ACTION PLANNING 1

IMPROVE INFORMATION TRANSFER BETWEEN COMPANY & CUSTOMER

What information do customers need to provide?

Could this information be more accurately and conveniently given online by customers?

What information could the company give to its customers?

What new information could be exchanged online?

For each, is it a better service for customers?

Is the new online service idea really compelling?

Is it enough in itself to bring customers online, and to get them to start exchanging information?

Will they tell friends and colleagues?

ACTION PLANNING 2

WHERE IS THE BEST ONLINE BUSINESS OPPORTUNITY?

Can the company's online service be built around the customer?

...their view of the company's products?

...their view of complementary products?

When customers purchase the company's product, what else are they buying at the same time, from your company and from its competitors?

What complementary goods are they buying to use with your products?

Is there an online marketplace where these goods are traded? Or can you share customers with those providing complementary services?

Make it easier for customers to buy all the products they need to use with yours, by working with these other suppliers.

What does the company need to change to compete effectively in open market spaces?

CHAPTER 4

HOW TO PROMOTE A COMPANY ONLINE

Now that the online store is live, how else can I build an online business?

What's the right level of investment?

There are 4 levels of company commitment to being online.

4   Sociable

3   Sales

2   Information Service

1   Passive presence

Customers don't yet know how they are going to use the online services that you offer them.

But online it's easier to see what works and what doesn't.

Expect to develop your services through rapid prototyping, development and obsolescence at each stage.

HOW SHOULD YOUR COMPANY INVEST IN ONLINE COMMERCE?

LEVEL ONE: BE PRESENT

Provide an online brochure. But don't simply transpose print artwork to web pages.

Online readers are be different from the people who read your printed literature. We all read differently online.

Bear in mind:

✦ fewer words will be required on each page, visible in a screen without the need to scroll

✦ pictures take a long time to download, so smaller images may change page layouts

✦ we read books from cover to cover whereas online we follow the most interesting link in a non-linear structure.

Organize website to have the content that customers most want to use placed most prominently.

That makes your site feel immediately easier to use, for the vast majority of customer.

LEVEL TWO: BE INFORMATIVE

Think of your website as a free-flowing, always-on, up-to-date information resource for customers. That's for customers - the site should always report information that's useful!

✦ home page highlights the most important news

✦ news pages report on latest product and services

✦ email newsletters add timely offers to registered customers

✦ RSS[3] feeds deliver your news automatically to readers who set it up.

LEVEL THREE: EASIER SALES

CUT FRICTION TO ADD PROFIT ON EVERY SALE

Removing the cost of processing a sale online adds value to each sale.

Think of the friction caused whenever a human is involved in selling. What's friction? It is the cost of the time taken and resources used every time a piece of information has to be handled by a human being. There's no friction in a sale that is handled completely online.

It does cost a business to remove friction:

---

[3] RSS - Really Simple Syndication - sends updated content from your site, straight to readers who ask for it

+ there's the actual cost of installing and integrating computer programs

+ managing the new roles that staff now play

+ the cost of working with customers to get the new system right

Weigh up how much friction it's worth removing!

FRICTIONLESS SALES;

DEVELOPMENT IN THREE STEPS

A business does not have to become a complete dot.com overnight.

Choose how much friction it is useful, appropriate and cost-effective to remove.

Balance those three questions by checking:

+ will our customers notice that we've changed?

+ will colleagues notice we've changed?

If either group won't notice, than why bother? Haven't you more important things to be doing!

Question 1. e-service: friction-free self-service information

Customers can search in their own time for product and pricing information, press coverage and reviews.

If the company keeps user manuals & support topics up-to-date, customers will self-serve their own solutions.

Question 2. digital marketing: friction-free transaction processing

An online front end to the existing business. Allow customers to assemble and pay for their orders online but use existing order handling systems for delivery.

There's no need to re-invent every process. The chances of success with minimal disruption are higher if changes are introduced gradually.

Question 3. e-business: friction-free order fulfillment and follow-up

Integrate all the processes into a single system in which all users of the system share the same information at the same time.

These tasks can be carried out in any order.

Every step has back-office and front-office components. Back office systems can be integrated quietly in private, without changing the front office. Front office changes are more noticeable and may have PR advantages.

✦ reducing the print, storage and wastage costs of product literature and manuals

✦ delivering information to customers, suppliers and distributors faster, for less

✦ allowing sales and distribution to develop with much lower capital (cash) investments

✦ improving management reporting, at higher speed and accuracy

CATER FOR EVERYBODY, NOT JUST ONLINE CUSTOMERS

Since not all customers will wish to complete an order online, give them with details of offline order systems.

These customers need order forms that they can complete onscreen, print off and fax or post.

And make sure that blank forms can be printed off too. For good measure, check that the printed layout flows well - it may be different from the onscreen layout.

& now test print... to be certain that the forms fit neatly on the printed page. There's little more wasteful in 21c life than one line of print that wastes an extra sheet of paper.

Place the sales team's phone or fax number in obvious places. Offer callback buttons... and out of office hours messaging services, by phone, on-screen form and email.

Customers who don't wish to order online may still be happy to browse a catalogue and then call to place their orders.

Don't forget about maps. If your business has shops, resellers, or service areas, map them! For customers who want to visit a shop, QR codes (to scan address & contact details into a cell phone) is a super-fast way to help them.

LEVEL FOUR: BE SOCIABLE

With the first three levels of commitment taken on board, building relationships is the natural next level of commitment. Throughout online channels, buyers, sellers, suppliers and distributors share information with each other to create smarter businesses.

If this is a sensible thing to do, for everybody, then it's natural to wish to repeat it.

Which social services are customers using? Follow their choice. Go and meet them on their own, virtual, social turf. Join customers where they're already comfortable, rather than askign them to take part in an official social space, elsewhere.

Today's relationship is next year's one night stand. Your company and its online network will have to work out a definition of a relationship. Together.

Little acts of generosity

What does a digital experience look like when it crops up in the real world?

It might be an apparently small, helpful innovation - like putting shopping baskets in the middle of a shop, where they're convenient for customers. How often do shoppers start with one or two items on their list, and find themselves, mid-store, with literally more than a handful of goods they want to buy. Retailers tend to put baskets by the tills, where it's convenient for the shop.

Online, they'd design the experience to be convenient for the shopper, because it's good for business.

Here's another.

How many coffee loyalty cards do you carry? Chances are that if you've any at all, then you've more than one. Which challenges the whole notion of loyalty. It's a discount card, pure & simple. And stallholders are prepared to stamp out the 6th cup free to any passing stranger.

So why don't they do exactly that? Carry on with the current system for regular customers, with their own collection cards. And stamp a shared card for every customer... keep that 'community card' behind the counter... and give every sixth stranger a free cup of coffee...

If you were stood on a rail terminus or High Street with a choice of coffee vendors, which one are you going to choose?

That would be the one that might give you a cup of coffee for free.

These little acts of generosity add a sprit of fun, of friendliness.

Make it easier to choose one shop over another

which would serve as a plain-speaking definition of what marketing is for.

ACTION PLANNING

Organize websites around the products and services that customers visit to use; put those seervices front & centre

Be the most up to date and accurate source of news about your company and products

Find ways to make online buying as easy as possible:

✦ let customers login with open format passwords - OpenId, Twitter & Facebook Connect

✦ use common Form Field names to encourage auto-filling

✦ make it easy to pay, with Paypal, Google Checkout & simple card processing setup

✦ let customers track their orders

Be sociable, by finding how your company's expertise can best guide customers & non-customers. Be equally open and helpful to both!

Seek out little acts of generosity:

✦ small gifts, that are valued by your customers, and that have little cost to the company.

CHAPTER 5
EFFECTIVE EMAIL MARKETING

MANAGING PERMISSION EMAIL

There are rules to follow about how to email your customers.

A visitor (who, remember, may not yet be a customer) gives his or her permission to receive email when you have harvested their email address (harvesting is described in 'The five business benefits of digital marketing'). But do not abuse that permission.

Make it very clear that:

✦ recipients control the relationship - why the email has been sent It is easy to stop future communications - there will be no further follow-up

✦ emails are sent only once - make a strong statement that visitor information will remain private

✦ recipients have the chance to update their information, and keep future emails relevant.

When you follow all of these guidelines correctly, recipients will be happy to receive email and will be more responsive.

The opposite of permission is spam.

Spam is the online term for unsolicited commercial email (the legal definition) or

"emails that I didn't ask for, from people I don't know, selling products I don't want"

That's most people's definition of spam.

Guard against email being treated as spam in three ways:

1. Legally   Did the recipient give formal permission to use their information?

2. Rationally   Is customer information being used in the way the company intended?

and disclosed when it was first captured?

3. Emotionally Will the recipients feel that they've been spammed?

There is no absolute definition of spam. Remember that the customer controls the relationship.

If the customer says it's spam, then it is spam.

Respect customer views.

It is spam when:

✦ The recipient's permission has "decayed".
If it's been a while since permission was given, or since the last email, the recipients may either have forgotten that they gave their permission or have withdrawn it.

✦ Permission is abused by writing too often.
Write when the company has news that'll interest the recipients.

✦ When there's no way to update a recipients subscription, or to unsubscribe.
The only defense against unintentionally spamming a customer is to have a clear and easy "unsubscribe" link in every email, and to make sure that customers who don,'t wish to receive emails never do.

✦ And check, does the use of customer information comply with local privacy legislation?

KEEP EMAILS ON MESSAGE

Once visitors understand who is writing to them, and are reminded that they gave their permission, your email will be greeted more warmly. And opened!

Building and maintaining the trust that you have created is vital. Keep emails on message: if permission was given to write with service information for product owners, don't let their emails become a list of "special" third-party offers.

EMAIL IS NOT ALL ABOUT WORDS

Most of us use email every day. We send simple text messages with documents attached. We might refer to a web page that the recipient should look at. Marketing email should be as carefully prepared as all our personal email:

Formats: some people prefer to read simple text email, while others prefer the graphic design of html formats - so send both.

It's particularly important to remember the text version if your customers are likely to open email on their cell phones. Not only is text quicker to load, it's unlikely to be scrambled on the display.

Spam filters can block bulk email before it reaches your customer. When customers register for email, ask to be added to their address book which 'whitelists' your email address. Then always send email from that address!

Link directly from your email to the relevant web pages. Place the links early in the email where more readers will see them!

Measure which links are clicked most and test to find which topics receive most clicks.

... now "do more" with those popular topics:

✦ Include those topics in future emails

✦ Make the popular topics easy to find in website navigation

✦ & include the key words of those popular topics in social activity - Facebook pages & Twitter.

THREE TYPES OF EMAIL

1 Text email

Stand-alone advertisements, sent to a list of people who have agreed to receive them

With clickable links to find out more or to register for an offer

2 Visual email

Laid out in the form of a web page

An effective way for a company to bring a website to its customers

Can include graphics and banner advertising, so may generate advertising sales revenue while providing a service to customers

3 Rich Media by email

Email messages, sent through ordinary email channels, that include graphics, sound, animation and video

Can be personalized and can include HTML and rich media sounds or moving images.

EMAIL DESIGN

SO YOU SEE WHAT I'M SAYING?

Recipients will have very slightly different display settings for their email. Prepare emails so that they have the best chance of being displayed as the designer intended:

✦ width of no more than 65 text characters

✦ use white space and simple formatting to give fast download speeds

✦ demonstrate you know the customer's perspective

✦ build rapport and personalize by speaking one to one

✦ ask recipients to forward the email to friends and colleagues

✦ put unsubscribe information early in the message

COMPELLING EMAIL COPY

Before the reader opens the message, the subject line, sender and, perhaps, the first lines of the message will be visible.

Make these details enticing so that the message is opened:

✦ place important information early in the message, before the reader has to scroll down

✦ avoid FREE! &c similar hype language as some email filter programs may block them

✦ if you're sending larger quantities of email, test different copy versions to find out which receive the highest:

  ✦ open rate

  ✦ clickthrough rate

  ✦ purchase rate, by number of customers and by $ value

USING EMAIL SIGNATURES EFFECTIVELY

An email signature at the end of a message is a powerful invitation for the reader to find out more.

✦ create a suite of signatures for different purposes

✦ be brief and to the point: 4-6 lines maximum, 60 characters in width

✦ include contact information online and offline (an email address and a relevant, clickable, URL) together with a brief benefit for the reader

✦ legally, an email is just another piece of company stationery, and needs only the same formal information as appears on a letterhead.

For powerful business strategy emails

ReadyNow@SpotOnThinking.com

www.SpotOnThinking.com

BUSINESS TO BUSINESS EMAIL GUIDELINES

Unless you're certain that recipients want long, colorful messages, stick to brief text messages!

Consider avoiding HTML for quicker downloads - remember your readers may be on their cell phone.

Research your lists; use test groups

Offer something free if you can to generate leads: product demonstrations, background papers, video demonstrations, limited-time exclusives deals, advance notice of events and offers, value-add offers or discounts...

If an offer is described as being a "web exclusive" or "email exclusive", then make sure it's exactly that, and not available elsewhere, at the time the email is sent.

Keep copy tight and to the point

Speak to audience in their language, using their buzzwords. Put at least three response links in the copy - start, body copy and end.

Personalize as much as possible.

Give recipients several opportunities to ask questions, make comments, and forward the message to their network, by email and social networks.

Send out midweek and avoid busy periods.

Make sure you can respond to the response!

Then do it all again - follow-up mails can be as
effective as the first communication

Action Planning

Respect permission!

Write interesting emails to customers but first ensure that they wish to receive them.

Write emails when there's news that customers will want to hear - and don't write if email content isn't interesting to customers.

Do find a voice that customers will recognize. Don't invent a corporate tone of voice that couldn't be used in real life.

Simpler design is most likely to be delivered as intended; personal email programs aren't able to check layout & appearance: use online services to manage 20 or more recipients.

Build-in measurements: check what works, and do it again next time.

Plan to repeat!

Email isn't a one-off; it works best as a follow up to earlier activity.

CHAPTER 6

SOCIAL MEDIA & PUBLIC RELATIONS

CUT OUT JOURNALISTS: GO STRAIGHT TO OPINION FORMERS

When we say "social media" we mainly mean Facebook & Twitter for 'all of us', Myspace for music, and LinkedIn for business.

Other social spaces happily co-exist, and should be included if that's where your customers hang out.

These social spaces look like they're a chance to drop tasty & enticing messages directly in front of prospective customers. That's true... and probably incidental to the bigger opportunity.

Discussions in Social channels

Word of mouth recommendations are the most powerful form of promotion - for and against companies.

Social media - mainly Facebook and Twitter - are an engine for online word of mouth marketing. But simply pitching up and setting up stall isn't the way to get the best out of time spent there. Besides, there are paid-for advertising services for that sort of approach.

Amongst your customers are a small number of opinion formers. Vocal customers, who have a following. Their opinions may or may not be factually correct.

The advantage of social conversations online is that the company can see what they're saying, and respond to it.

[& yes, however ludicrous, prejudiced, and biased these opinion formers are, a level-headed response is better than none at all.]

How do I find out who matters?

It's not all about who has the most Likes on Facebook, or Followers on Twitter.

✦ who's opinions are repeated most often?

✦ are they willing to 'play along' and use their network to support the company's efforts?

✦ who will get into a useful conversation with the company, and held feedback the customer experience, good & bad?

A Google search for the company name or product name will include social status updates: who regularly posts & rank high in results.

Equally useful, a # hashtag search will turn up folk discussing competitor products as well.

Check their reputation on a service like PeerIndex:

✦ follow the thoughts of the most useful

✦ comment on & repeat their posts

✦ don't hesitate to make direct contact

✦ keep the tone positive!

✦ remember that anything you've written can be reposted in a different context.

Follow, friend, like my company because...

Over ten years ago a quartet of wise men wrote http://cluetrain.com - which cemented the idea that "markets are conversations". Very true - and if your company were to join a conversation, what would it say? How would it sound? What would the company bring to the conversation that the folk listening will find interesting, and want to take away... to share in their other conversations?

The success trick for social is to bring something interesting or useful to the party.

The more interesting your status, the more useful it is, the more likely folk are to share it.

Simple ideas work best. Share news about New product, B Grade stock on sale, photos of the Company team at work, traveling, at play.

Not every status update is a sales message - perhaps only 1 in 10 mentions product. Maybe fewer; your conversations will find the level that's right for your audience.

Keep it real, and at a personal level.

So when listing (for example) B Grade stock for sale, have some that are just 1 item per update; showing both price & discount. Then readers get the whole story in 140 characters .

Pick out hero products as examples of what's available, for readers to find and share.

Going large; automated updates and social Public Relations

How we talk changes with the number we're talking to. One-to-one chats and meetings are very different from a large audience of 150. Social updates have the illusion of being one to one, even when read by hundreds, or thousands.

When audiences grow past 150, that's more than the natural number of real life contacts - see: en.wikipedia.org/wiki/Dunbar's_number

For these larger audiences, change how your company's social marketing works. The audience that's been built up may expect a flow of updates, in the morning, during the day, or evening, So consider how to best balance activity across your followers' active day.

Readers don't stay online all day, so it may be useful to schedule updates that follow their sun from East coast to West, and the far shores of the Atlantic to Pacific.

Mix real time posts with pre-scheduled content.

Simply re-posting today's real-time updates so they're freshly available for readers later... which may of course, with time shifts, mean that a 'first thing in the morning post' is published as 3, 4 or even 5 timezones wake up.

So take care that in making an effort to share the good stuff with everybody, it doesn't look like groundhog day!

A web resource for journalists

Online, your public relations is a different job from traditional PR.

Activity can become highly interactive since the company is much closer to its customers and opinion formers.

Journalists work to tight deadlines. Press releases can get greater coverage by being available online, from where journalists can download extra, last-minute copy.

Provide editors and journalists with discrete areas of a company website. Give them the facility to download unformatted ASCII text versions of your press releases and to download low-, medium- and high- resolution photos to accompany stories.

NEWSGROUPS & MESSAGE BOARDS

Joining and actively participating in a customer discussion list is a good way to meet key opinion-formers. Many groups are long established as boards & email lists, and haven't migrated to sociable platforms.

Frank and open opinions are the engine of these online spaces, and the quality of discussion is usually very high; you'll often find opinion formers here, er, forming their opinions!

Consequently they are very good for getting feedback on what customers think about your products. Journalists often use discussion lists for article research.

'Off social' groups are likely to be quite protective of their membership. Don't attempt to participate without declaring your interest; pitched right, there's every chance the group will welcome your expert insight & perspective.   If they don't want you, it's not a huge deal. Shrug your shoulders & move on.

To get the best from online groups:

Be clear about objectives. Are you researching, publicizing or informing and educating?

Introduce yourself carefully: lurk and get a feel before being open about your interest in the group. Use an email signature. Then subscribe and actively participate. Share expertise and knowledge with the group.

Respect the culture and personalities within the group. Be prepared to apologize if you cause offense.

ACTION PLANNING

Find social content about your products, company & markets:

look for the problems that customers have, which are solved by company product

Who's reputable, and leading the conversations?

work with them

Find small & frequent news that's interesting for customers:

post it!

Put the web & social addresses on every communication, from letterheads to advertising

Find out how the company site could help journalists and public relations agents

CHAPTER 7
DIGITAL ADVERTISING

FOUR FORMS OF ONLINE ADVERTISING

Online advertising can be a cost-effective way to bring traffic to your site and sell specific products or events. There are four principal types of advert:

1. Text advertising: displayed alongside search results, in newsletters and community forums.

2. Banner ads: still and moving images placed on web pages in prominent positions by advertising sales houses and by search engines.

3. Pop-up windows: advertising in a new window which may appear over or under the current browser window.

4. Video adverts: made possible by broadband; add sound and motion for extra impact.

BUYING AND PUBLISHING ONLINE
ADVERTISING

Pay per Click services (from Google, Yahoo! Facebook, LinkedIn & more) is the most common way of buying small-scale classified advertising.

The publishers figure out what your ad is for, by reading it & the page it points to, and publish the ad alongside relevant pages - search engine results, professional editorial, or personal pages.

There's also a number of market-specific advertising networks, that carry ads for one interest group. If your target industry has one, it'll be more expensive to use, and should deliver more cost-effective results.

How to set up pay per click ads

✦ once you've set up an account, write your text advertisement, or upload your image ad

✦ choose a page for click-throughs to land on that's relevant to the ad (or create one)

✦ select the search keywords that you think customers will use to find products like yours

✦ choose a maximum bid for each keyword

✦ add analysis code to the landing pages at the start & end of your checkout process

There's plenty of tools to help at each stage.

Now, try to cut down the number of times ads appear by localizing geography.

Next, try to put ads in front of potential customers at times of day that they'll be online.

Retargeting: smart ads that follow visitors

Wouldn't it be smart if visitors to a store found they saw more of that store's advertising in the days and weeks after?

The store could concentrate its ad budget on the hottest prospects - folk in the market to buy its products right now.

The customer sees a higher proportion of ads from a store they know, and are interested in buying from... which could make a small company appear to be far larger, and a much bigger spender than it is in reality.

'Retargeting' service companies offer campaigns starting from $10s (& of course Google offers retargeting as an extension to its advertising services. The ads are offered on a Pay per Click basis - it cost the company nothing to display that ads - and a charge is only made when the viewer clicks on the banner. Of course, since the viewer is a hot prospect, that click will be more expensive than a less well targeted ad would have been.

So that would be the perfect form of advertising, wouldn't it?

✦ shown only to recent store visitors

✦ free until the decide to click & come back

✦ & since they're hot returning visitors, a sale is more likely.

It would be perfect, if it weren't abused! Large online stores don't seem to care enough about how their customers feel about their brands, and allow ad agents to serve ads to customers who either aren't interested... or to display the wrong ads.

Cookies make ad retargeting work

Cookies are simple text files, downloaded from a webpage, and store on the visitor's computer. The cookies record information that's useful to the visitor - automatic login & the visitor's product preferences, for example - and can note information useful to the company as well - usually which pages were visited.

It's these page visits that trigger retargeted ads. Visiting an 'On Sale' page ought to trigger ads for (you guessed it) our Sale.

To avoid retargeting turning into stalking (!) try to:

✦ understand a typical customer's buying cycle: if most customers buy after two visits, and within 10 days of the first visit, then set retargeting to stop shortly after that time.

✦ use a range of retargeting cookies to reflect the product range that the visitor was interested in. An Auto shop selling parts, cleaning accessories, and baby seats could tag each range differently, and show customers ads relevant to their shopping interests

✦ take note when a visitor puts goods into their shopping cart... and leaves them there!

Set three cookies inside the shopping cart:

1. 'started shopping' cookie the first time a product goes into the cart,

2. 'checkout' cookie when the visitor stops browsing and started paying

3. and finally a 'finished shopping' cookie on the 'Thank You' page.

This isn't any different from the things a shop assistant would say to a customer as they move around the store.

And the retargeting ads can reflect those same thoughts:

1. "Hey, thanks. That's great. What else can we get you?"

2. "Have you seen our special offers if you checkout today?"

3. "Hey, thanks for shopping with use. Come back soon"

Improving your ads

Getting ads up & running is just the start! The ad services will allow you to set a daily budget; aim low at first, and expand the budget once it's proven to deliver profitable sales.

It's very quick & easy to try different versions of headlines, offers, ad copy, and landing url. Test one variation at a time though, so that you can always tell which alteration caused the improvement.

If online enquiries & sales are important to your business, it'll be worth spending some time testing different versions of adverts and landing pages, to see which work best.

In order of likely impact on response, test;

1 Timing: what time of day, or day of week, is most effective at getting interest & sales?

2 Targeting: who is most responsive to adverts? What (online) keywords attract their attention, and where are they in the real world?

3 Offer: does an added-value offer receive more interest than a discount? Is a limited supply more engaging than a time-limited offer?

4 Creative   what's the most effective form of words to wrap up Timing, Targeting and the Offer into a compelling pitch? Different versions may work for each group of customers & products.

Use analysis tracking code to check which ads produce most visits, registrations, highest number and value of sales, and the most profit.

Publishing ads on your website

You can publish commission-earning advertising on your website. Search engines and affiliate advertising services will deliver adverts that are relevant to your page content.

Reader numbers need to be very high to make any significant income from most indirect sellers - if earnings were $0.5 per thousand, would your business be able to make better use of the space?

Direct sellers are a different matter, as they can offer much higher income. Though of course to make it worth their while, the advertisers will need to be interested in *exactly* the audience that's on your site.

Putting ads on your pages

Ad serving is as simple as adding some code from a 3d party partner. Google (of course) has a service, as does openX.org.

1.Getting started with either is as simple as: Signing Up.

2.Setting some filters to reflect the kind of ads you'd like to display.

3.Pasting the code provided into your web pages.

Both will manage the entire process on your behalf, while giving you the option to run internal house and direct sale ads amongst their inventory.

ACTION PLANNING

Make online graphics and copy messages consistent with all other media

Test different channels - Search & Publisher

Test different offers - eg extra free vs free delivery

In Pay per Click, test headlines, body copy & tailored landing URL

Measure the effectiveness of each initiative at bringing in valuable customers

Set retargeting cookies to display ads that are relevant to what your visitors were doing when they left the store

Set a budget! Concentrate on what advertising is earning, as well as its costs

CHAPTER 8

MANAGING SEARCH ENGINES

GETTING THE BEST FROM SEARCH ENGINES

Search engines drive traffic to your web pages: between 50% and 80% of traffic will come from a handful of major search engines.

Facebook may receive more attention from customers, while they're being sociable with each other; that doesn't stop search engines being important when folk shop online!

The three steps to decent search engine visibility are:

1. Use a Content Management System that's friendly to search engines.

2. Write content that customers would expect to find, in language they'll use.

3. Write about company products, services, events and news, anywhere else that's relevant.

4. Check what works, and do more of it to improve.

When we say 'search engine optimization', we generally mean Google. After a decade dominating search, it's not surprising that Google has become very good at spotting and discounting the professionals who set out to cheat the system. For a while it was relatively easy to mislead the results ranking, using 'black hat' techniques to boost the traffic to a site on false basis.

It's now very hard to cheat Google; 'white hat' - honest optimization - is the way to go. For many businesses that's no more than common sense steps to help engines do their work accurately.

Engines find websites by spidering the internet: software spiders cross the web, looking for content to index. So it,'s very, very (very!) important to build a website which spiders can read.

Spiders like pages which:

✦ make it easy to understand what a page is about, because spiders use the same words as folk searching on the subject (keywords)

✦ are fresh with recent updates (that would be news, blog posts, and social updates

✦ form part of a network of reputable sites on the same topic

REPUTATION COUNTS

A site's reputation matters plenty in figuring out it's prominence in search results. A search engine's way of figuring out reputation is to look at the sites in its network - and in particular the highly reputable sites that link to, quote and cite it.

Social media back-links count in that reputation process, as do social bookmarks and url-shorteners, blog comments and community forum posts. Each contributes to a site's stance in a network.

The freshness of links is a factor too - so just as a site is 'rewarded' in search results for being in place a long time, having a network of fresh referring links ads to the reputation.

USING A PAGE ADDRESS TO MAKE
PAGES VISIBLE

The UniqueResourceLocator is the address typed into a web browser's toolbar. Search engines will use it to answer their users' searches.

Your company name may be the first thing that visitors look for, therefore it makes sense to own yourcompanyname.com

Alternatively think of what visitors would search for. It is quick and easy to register related URLs, if you can find one that's available. A floor mop company might register, for example, FloorMop.~, CleanFloors.~ or MrsMop.~.

As soon as these are registered they can be directed at an existing company web page.

Name your pages in the same way - with real words and not a meaningless character string - to make pages more visible.

Avoid page addresses that include query variables like ? or = as they can divert search spiders.

MANAGE TAGS TO RECEIVE MORE VISITORS

What are they?

Descriptions of your site that appear in search engine results. Most CMS (Content Management Systems) will generate suggestions for each of these. They're usually a good starting point, and ready for improvement by a human that's familiar with the company and its customers.

Every piece of content that's added to the site should be tagged with relevant, natural-language tags - the words that visitors would use to summarize that piece of content.

Why are they so important?

Search engine spiders use tags to help decide how relevant your content is to a search:

Write 'tags that work' by keeping to the natural language that your visitors would use, and:

✦ write your page's title, description and content keywords

✦ make sure that headings (H1) and sub-headings (H2, H3) include relevant tags

✦ hyperlink to any page text that's important enough to have its own page

PUT SERVICE OUT AMONGST CUSTOMERS

Now that you have a good idea of which keyword tags are used by customers when they're talking about products, and have added them to site pages... Get out amongst the community of potential customers, and write. Customer support is the most productive place to start.

Encouraging customers to share their experiences - good & otherwise - is an opportunity to respond, in public, in a keyword rich conversation.

Since customers will have those conversations whether you're involved or not, it's best to get involved:

✦ sort out customer issues, and discuss how they arose & can be prevented

✦ take and share the praise for great service.

SEVEN IMPORTANT WRITING CONCEPTS

1. When writing use terms that visitors searching for products will use, regardless of whether or not they know your company.

2. Brands' product brand names (yours, not competitors)

3. Company names (the current and previous names)

4. Names of well-known staff - from the CEO through to local sales representatives

5. Words common to your industry: jargon, ISO standards, regulations, legislation, trade bodies...

6. Phrases in common use, from advertising strap lines to the language used in company literature

7. And generic product descriptors, that are not trade names belonging to other companies. Only use 970 Txi TurboSpeed if it's one of your products.

WRITING WITH KEYWORDS

Search spiders are very, very good at spotting a site that's pretending to be something that it isn't - so don't pretend!

Be yourself, write in natural language, not jargon, and use the same vocabulary that your customers use.

Give each page its own title: don't be cryptic, or use puns; call a spade a spade.

Longer page copy makes it easier for search spiders to understand your content, so make each page on your site a complete story: aim for over 200 words per page.

Observe and experiment by using your activity reports to see which copy and pages attract most visitors.

ACCESSIBLE PAGES ARE EASY TO SPIDER

Your website should be accessible to visually-impaired visitors. There is a set of standards designed to work with screen readers which change the look of a page into high-contrast easy-to-read text. You'll find that this builds a web page with navigation that is easy for every visitor to use:

✦ clearly named headings and images

✦ consistent look to navigation

✦ consistent behavior from links

This makes your page easy to understand, and users won't have unexpected results when they click on a link.

Check your site's compatibility with international standards at www.w3.org/WAI/ER/tools.

There's an added bonus - an accessible page is also easy for search engines to spider.

WHERE DO VISITORS COME FROM?

Chances are that your website will make more sales if more folk visit - so it's important to understand where visitors come from and how they found you. Website analysis tools will tell you if it was via a:

+ link from another site (which one?)

+ search engine (which one and which particular search word or phrase?)

While you can expect half of all visitors to leave after looking at your Home page (it wasn't what they were looking for!) what did the other half do?

WHAT DO VISITORS DO ON YOUR SITE?

Use a web analysis tool to check if visitors are following expected routes through your site. Do they come in the front door (Home page), look at some products and leave by the checkout?

Can you see common behavior amongst visitors who left without becoming customers?

What products were left in shopping carts? Which pages did visitors leave from? Try changing these pages to encourage visitors to follow your routes through the shop.

Are your most important pages (for example, top selling product pages, shopping cart pages and 'Thank you for your purchase" pages) the most popular ones? If they aren't, which pages are your visitors going to?

WELL-NETWORKED PAGES GET MORE TRAFFIC

Grow traffic by placing your pages at the centre of a network of relevant pages: find ways to place links back to your pages from industry websites, blogs and relevant forum pages.

If one page appears to draw more search traffic than others, try to understand why:

✦ check its Page Rank (one of the factors in Google,'s results calculation, and visible on the Google toolbar). On a scale of 0-10, ranks of 4-6 are healthy and likely to contribute to visibility

✦ check on the page's inbound links (it,'s a measure of a page's place in the network).

With most search engines, search on: 'links: url'.

UPDATE PAGES REGULARLY TO KEEP THEM VISIBLE

Search engines like websites that are kept fresh with regular updates, and generally rank them higher than older sites.

Blogging software is designed to create up-to-date pages that spider very easily. Your company blog might include:

✦ product and service updates

✦ staff announcements

✦ industry news and comment

Whichever pages you choose to update, try to show those updates as headlines on your Home page.

LEARN FROM COMPETITORS!

The web thrives on transparency - don,'t be shy about checking how competitors build and promote their online business.

Use a search engine to look for your services, and review competitors,' results

Check competitors,' page titles and descriptions: are they good descriptions of your business?

Use the 'links: url' search to see which sites link to top-ranking competitors

Does paid advertising display alongside a search for your business name? Should you be paying for similar advertising?

JUST A FEW MEASUREMENTS

There are so many different statistics that can be measured, consequently the only practical way to manage your site is to look for changes to normal traffic patterns.

To do this you need to first find out what 'normal,' looks like. Select a small number of items, your 'top 10',that you wish to keep track of and then monitor these on a regular basis. Those items are likely to include:

+ entry pages

+ routes through your site

+ exit pages

+ abandoned shopping carts - volume, value and key products

+ sales - volume, value and key products

+ search terms

Since most traffic will enter through the Home page, keep a close eye on where visitors go to next.

AND FINALLY, MOMENTUM

Many search engines favor sites that rank highly in previous searches and that were clicked upon.

The better the rankings a site achieves, the more the engine will do to keep it at this level.

This makes it tougher to break into the top results. But once a page makes it to the top, it will be more visible in search results, be visited more often and quickly becomes harder to dislodge.

Get a page up there.

The effort repays itself.

ACTION PLANNING

Is the site designed to be search-engine friendly?

Are meta tags and alt tags in place?

- Check that they are the right tags for your company.

- Search for a meta tag generator if you're not sure.

Take a turn around the search loop!

1 Check analytics to find the most common search terms

2 Search for the site - with those top search terms - as if you're a customer. If it's not top of the search, figure out what your higher-placed competitors did to earn their ranking.

3 Make some improvements. Try changing one thing on each page.

Monitor inbound links.

Update the site's content regularly.

CHAPTER 9

MANAGING CUSTOMER SERVICE TO CREATE TRUST

Last & far from least, trust, security & data protection are the final hurdles to get over before actually making some money... which is usually the whole point of business.

There's a few simple steps that can make the difference between making a sale and another abandoned shopping cart. Mostly they're about being transparent with your customers, making sure that they're as comfortable as possible with the checkout, delivery and returns procedures.

Ideally, they'll be so comfortable that customers will never pause to think about the cost or timing of their delivery, and will get straight on with the business of paying.

MAKE YOUR SECURITY APPROPRIATE

Every website needs the right level of security for the information that is being protected. A dime widget store needs a lot less security than a bank.

Ensure that customers do not feel inhibited, delayed or inconvenienced by any security process. But do protect yourself from customers.

Mostly the information a customer needs to give to complete their transaction is itself enough security - name, email address and a street address. Along with payment information that works for the honest customer. And to add anything further to the checkout process risks losing sales.

To add security, many organizations insert a Captcha code as the last step before submitting a form or payment. Captchas present the customer with distorted pictures of letters & numbers. The intention is that automated form submission robots can't read the picture, so aren't able to complete the sale. The actual result is the many real people can't read the form, and sales & registrations are lost.

Fraud is a real issue, and should be considered carefully! Payment providers give the best defense by identifying fraudulent behavior patterns. But it's very hard for retailer or payment provider to protect against credit or debit card information being stolen - the rightful owner still has their card - and the details entered correctly by a thief. Until the card owner reports the "things I didn't buy on my statement", or the thief overuses the card, it's quite difficult to stop.

Companies with digital products are most at risk. Inserting an "email confirmation" step into your sales process, before issuing a product code, is one of the few things that can be done to discourage fraud on a digital product. [Fraudsters are good at nailing Captcha codes, so they don't add much defense].

To reduce multiple fraudulent sales to the same thief, set the sales approval database to identify any duplicated email addresses, and have those checked manually before products are released to the customer Requiring fraudsters to set up multiple email addresses - one for each sale - makes it more difficult, and takes much longer per 'sale' - so they're more likely to leave your business alone.

SECURE YOUR SITE INTERNALLY & EXTERNALLY

What levels of authentication do you need?

How do your customers know that they are looking at your web pages? And how does your website know that customers are who they say they are?

What information do you have if a customer says they did not make an order or the goods were not delivered?

Worldwide most web users have access to 128 bit encryption versions of their web browsers.

This was until recently banking-level security. It is, therefore, likely to be good enough for any transactions a company will ask its customers to make.

Most payments take place behind a Secure Socket Layer - the locked padlock browser area. This is usually a more heavily fire-walled area of your web server.

A company's biggest security threat will not come from outside your organization.

Research shows that most security breaches are internal. Consequently, you should ensure that internal controls are installed alongside an external firewall.

Simple procedures often work best to protect from internal fraud & theft:

✦ change passwords from time to time, and store them securely, away from drives with network access

✦ don't store passwords in a file called "Passwords" - that just makes it too easy for search tools to find!

WEBSITE & VISITOR VERIFICATION

Do you know who you're talking to? It is relatively easy to become anonymous online or to assume a different persona. In extreme & rare cases, malicious people may even temporarily steal a site's identity.

It is important to be able to authenticate that a website is what it claims to be and visitors are genuinely who they say they are. Site authentication from organizations like Verisign give visitors a one-click check that a site is who & what it claims to be.

The simplest way for a website to confirm that customers are genuine is to have a system of user identification - usually passwords and personal data that customers enter to identify themselves.

CUSTOMER TRANSACTION RECORDS

Since the dawn of time mail order companies have struggled with customers who claim that something was missing from their order. Online services have the extra headache of customers claiming that goods have been charged to their accounts in error.

TRUST

Trust is a dynamic process for most consumers. Trust deepens or retreats depending on our experiences of dealing with suppliers. It's the same online as in the high street, though online we only have the images on an electronic screen to judge a company by.

Before we trust an organization, we look for rational and emotional indicators.

Emotionally, we look for behaviors such as manners, professionalism and sensitivity.

Rationally, formal claims to trustworthiness such as dependability, reliability and honesty reassure us.

And we look for visible signs of security.

FIVE WAYS TO BUILD TRUST ONLINE

1. CONSISTENT PRESENTATION

The look of a site conveys a sense of personality and influences the degree to which visitors are prepared to trust the site owner.

If an organization already has a brand identity then the site should be consistent with this. On-screen design and copy styles should reflect existing printed literature.

A company's colors may need re-working online, to a new palette that is fast to download to the computer screen.

Developing a brand to work online is a new task. The internet is tactile - web pages should look, sound and move in ways that reinforce the company's existing image.

2. VISITORS DECIDE NAVIGATION PRIORITIES

If customers walk into a new high street shop they can usually find their way around.

There are conventions for laying out a shop and customers unconsciously understand and follow them. Online sops are no different!

On the home page a site's purpose must be clear to the first-time visitor. The vast majority - up to 95% of visitors - are likely to visit for one purpose. Make it prominent, obvious, and easy to find. (Yes, that's the same thing, three time over - it really is that important!)

Use the same words to describe the site's content that your visitors use - even if it's not exactly how those things would be described inside the company.

Make it easy for visitors to find what they are looking for by giving clear instructions; don't hide commonly sought-after pages in drop down menus.

Follow the most common layout conventions:

✦ navigation links at top and bottom of pages

✦ images and buttons in the same place on each page

✦ text hyperlinks underlined in blue

Of course it's fine to be unconventional! If customers are prepared for the unexpected, then being different may boost sales.

3. TRANSPARENT FULFILLMENT

Goods have now been selected and your customer has made it to the checkout. At this point many shopping carts are abandoned.

Companies can keep customers' trust by taking them through a transparent transaction process. At all times customers should know where they are in the checkout process and they should be able to find out what happens later. It must be easy to see:

✦ delivery charges

✦ how orders are to be processed

✦ the company's returns policy

✦ online and offline customer support services

✦ ohe company's security policy for personal information

If you have shops on the high street, give customers the option to return goods there. And remember to train your staff to handle returned online orders.

4. WE TRUST FAMILIAR NAMES & LOGOS

Names that we know and trust are familiar and friendly. If we see them on a website we trust the website more.

Customers trust sites where they can see the familiar logos of credit card brands, major software companies and web security organizations. If your company is trusted by these organizations, don't hide it.

Should your company have a familiar name, use it to build customer expectation of the site's content, the quality of products and the level of service support. Web customers will have higher service expectations than offline customers. They may expect service delivered in real time, with transparency and, above all, with consistency.

5. USE AS LITTLE TECHNOLOGY AS POSSIBLE

Too much technology can be daunting. Use technology as a transparent aid to navigation and activity. Aim for graphics and functions in proportion to your customer's needs. These needs will change with your customer's experience.

Are you handling visitors new to the web trade or devotees?

✦ newcomers need signposts

✦ old hands need quick routes to every part of the site.

✦ younger visitors and technically literate customers will tolerate more complex sites

✦ make sure that technology supports your sales process and does not obscure it:

✦ automatically recognize returning customers

✦ help to complete forms correctly

✦ use standard form field names, so that browser programs can automatically add a visitor's details.

SIX WAYS TO LOSE CUSTOMER TRUST

Make these mistakes and your customers will disappear fast:

1. Have out of date 'news' on a News page. And social services that aren't used.

2. Ignore customer emails. Folk expect a brisk answer.

3. Copy & paste a standard & wrong reply to a customer's email. It's a great way to show the company doesn't care, & is quite likely to be reposted just where the company wouldn't wish to see it.

4. cc customers on an email, and show their email address to other customers. Don't make a customer's personal details public. Ever.

5. Don't deal with negative comments on blog posts & in social media. Acknowledge & respond, or the bad image becomes reality.

6. Never pretend that a mistake didn't happen. Always 'fess up, before anybody else finds out.
                    They *will* find out.
When customers spot a problem, thank them, and share it. Then be open about how it's going to be repaired.

Notice that these are *all* small mistakes.

They can be made in a moment, or fixed with a moment's care. None of them is expensive to get right, nor do they take time, money & skill to avoid.

DATA PROTECTION

Data protection legislation now applies to personal data gathered online, which generally means that data should:

✦ be handled within the company by identifiable individuals or officers

✦ not be sent to unlicensed organizations for processing (for example, to send out emails)

✦ not be exported across national boundaries, unless to a 'safe' company with comparable protection in place.

COLLECTING & USING IMPERSONAL DATA AT A SINGLE SITE

Online, a name or even an email address is not essential to build up a profile.

Tracking an individual visitor during a visit to a website can build an informative profile of their interests. This is unlikely to cause offense if the details are not attached to information from other sources.

It is relatively easy to:

✦ inform your visitors of the tracking that is carried out on a company site

✦ explain the advantages

✦ seek permission to use tracking information to personalize users' visits

ACTIONS TO PROTECT DATA THAT IS

GATHERED ONLINE

Four simple steps to safeguard data collection and use

1 Companies must not sell information collected from cookies to third parties.

2 Nor must they track sensitive information such as medical information and financial information (creditworthiness).

3 Companies should provide consumers with notice and choice about internet advertising.

4 They must disclose their data collection and use practices on their websites in a clear, concise and conspicuous manner. They must disclose:

✦ what visitor information was captured and subsequently retained or deleted

✦ how data is used

✦ what opt-in or opt-out procedures are available to the visitor

ACTION PLANNING

LEGAL ISSUES

The law is coming to terms with digital marketing at a different rate in each country. Although the web is global, judgements vary from one jurisdiction to another. Ask your local legal advisers for their views.

Who is responsible for what is said in a chat room? If it is the people chatting, who are they? Or does the company that provides the chat space publish its content and take responsibility?

What rights and responsibilities do employers have for the contents of employees' computers?

In a global communications medium, which advertising law applies?

In Europe, the policy is that advertising and products from European companies must comply with domestic legislation.

Is the company registered for the appropriate data protection legislation?

Chapter 10
Eight Steps to Plan Successful Ecommerce

1 LET THE CUSTOMER PLAN

Digital Marketing

Good plans are simple plans. They are also measurable, their implementation is accountable, the resources to deliver the plan are available and there is a time-frame for the plan to be delivered.

Done.

Not quite. Whatever planning process an organization uses, expect that the company will not control the direction in which online services evolve.

Then your customer will decide what works and what doesn't.

2   RESPOND FAST

If the plan is to respond to customer wishes, then the most successful plan will be the one that responds fastest.

This means that every component of the plan should be built with the intention of proving a principle.

Ask yourself if your customers want this?

If they do, then a more robust version can be built.

If they don't, then you can redirect your time and resources and use the knowledge gained to good effect elsewhere.

3   TEST OUT YOUR PLAN

In the online marketplace everything is a test until it's proven by the customer.

Successful testing follows a simple rule:

Test one thing at a time.

Only test changes that can be measured directly. If a test includes more than one change, it's almost always impossible to measure the effect of each one.

Test to learn from the customer and to improve one step at a time.

4   CHALLENGE INTERNAL ASSUMPTIONS

Remove internal processing costs to make dramatic improvements to profit margins.

Analyze each part of the sales process to clarify what it is that staff spend time doing. In particular, look for processes in which information is transferred.

✦ How many steps can be eliminated by outsourcing tasks to your customers and suppliers?

✦ Who is best placed to make the original information entry?

✦ Can that information be shared to avoid re-entering the same information?

✦ What information could customers, suppliers and distributors find for themselves, computer to computer?

✦ With the time saved, what could your staff do to add more value for customers?

5   FOCUS ON CUSTOMER, SUPPLIER & DISTRIBUTOR BENEFITS

What's in it for customers, suppliers and distributors?

Have you asked what they'd like?

The web's very good at research. Are you offering them a new way to use an existing service or a completely new service?

Is it faster, cheaper, more convenient or just new and online?

What new information do they get?

Decide what you can reliably offer each group now and plan a phased introduction of more complex services.

Complexity often arises from integrating tried and tested stand-alone services.

6   GIVE GOOD REASONS TO USE ONLINE SERVICES

Not all customers will automatically move to an online service simply because it's there.

Equally, in a service's early stages it may not make good sense to risk overwhelming a new online channel by quickly moving large numbers of customers over to the new service.

If you prefer customers to use an online channel, find ways to:

✦ Inform them that it is there (they may not know this)

✦ Tell them how to change over

✦ Incentivize the swap to make it worthwhile

✦ Introduce the new service as a special privilege, beta test program

7   CALCULATE THREE SETS OF COSTS

Very few organizations have all the resources in-house to start offering online services.

There are three sets of costs that should be calculated:

1. Current company costs that will be altered by the online changes

✦ both internal and external costs

2. Cost to implement the changes

✦ interim support may be needed

✦ training for staff whose tasks change

3. New cost assumptions, post change

✦ long-term cost-savings

✦ long-term outsourcing arrangements

✦ ongoing online development plans

8 HELP STAFF ADAPT TO ONLINE

WORKING

An online service will affect your staff and the work that they do.

If your organization is typical, there will be a progressive transfer from processing tasks towards customer service.

Some may find this work more fulfilling; others will not enjoy the increased interaction with customers.

Unless a company's online services are entirely online, staff who are to fulfill new service roles will require assistance to develop new skills.

They will almost certainly require some training in how to make the most of the new technology for the benefit of their customers.

WHERE TO GO ONLINE TO FIND OUT MORE

Networks are an important part of the new economy.

Readers of this book have their own network. Join us at www.DigitalMarketingManual.com

It's a space in which you can share with other managers around the world your ideas, experiences and the challenges of managing digital marketing.

ABOUT THE AUTHOR

Will Rowan

Will is an experienced digital marketing consultant and trainer, with roots in blue-chip direct marketing. Since 1998 his consultancy TheCustomer has provided new marketing technologies training and consultancy to top five UK direct marketing agencies, leading travel and travel incentive companies, major banks, building societies, insurers, educational bodies and recruitment organizations.

Clients use TheCustomer for practical advice in exploiting new network technologies to make businesses more profitable:

! Strategic advice to business on the consequences of new technologies for customer communications and company structure

! Restructuring companies, communications and customer service activities to profit from customer information

! Identifying opportunities to improve business processes by applying customer information in real time

Will lives on the edge of the New Forest where he cycles, walks and occasionally works from a highly portable office. Readers may reach Will at Ask@TheCustomer.co.uk

www.ingramcontent.com/pod-product-compliance
Lightning Source LLC
Chambersburg PA
CBHW051546170526
45165CB00002B/904